BEDTIME SLEEP MEDITATIONS FOR CHILDREN

Guided Night Time Short Stories To Help Toddlers & Kids Fall Asleep At Night, Relax, And Have Beautiful Dreams

Author: Sleepy Willow

Copyright 2021 – All rights reserved.

The content contained within this book may not be reproduced, duplicated or transmitted without direct written permission from the author or the publisher.

Under no circumstances will any blame or legal responsibility be held against the publisher, or author, for any damages, reparation, or monetary loss due to the information contained within this book. Either directly or indirectly.

Legal Notice:

This book is copyright protected.

This book is only for personal use. You cannot amend, distribute, sell, use, quote or paraphrase any part, or content within this book, without the consent of the author or publisher.

Disclaimer Notice:

Please not the information contained within this document is for educational and entertainment purposes only.

No warranties of any kind are declared or implied. Readers acknowledge that the author is not engaging in the rendering of legal, financial, medical or professional advice.

The content within this book has been derived from various sources. Please consult a licensed professional before attempting any techniques outlined in this book.

By reading this document, the reader agrees that under no circumstances is the author responsible for any losses, direct or indirect, which are incurred as a result of the use of the information contained within this document, including, but not limited to: errors, omissions, or inaccuracies.

Table of content

Introduction 1

Chapter 1 3
   The Confident Mermaid Adventure 3

Chapter 2 14
   The Magic Carpet Ride 14

Chapter 3 23
   The Fairy Forest 23

Chapter 4 30
   Rapunzel And Believing 30

Chapter 5 40
   The Sleepy Animal Kingdom 40

Chapter 6 71
   The Magic Unicorn Adventure 71

Chapter 7 102
   Great Undersea Friends 102

Conclusion 111

INTRODUCTION

Thank you for listening and choosing *Bedtime Sleep Meditations For Children*.

In this magical and wonderful book, you will be taken on many adventures and listen to wonderful stories that will help you to fall asleep peacefully every night. I hope that you and your children will have hours of fun listening to these stories. Each story in this book will be entertaining and will have small lessons that your child can learn from. You will learn many skills that can help you relax your mind and body, so you have the most amazing sleep every night. Each story contains valuable lessons while relieving stress. Each story will empower you and your children to improve your self-confidence and self-esteem. You will learn how to deal with your emotions better and communicate them more effectively.

Children who experience lots of nightmares might be scared to fall asleep at night and might have a hard time relaxing at night because they are afraid of scary dreams. This book will help you combat and get rid of those fears. Each story will help you feel more relaxed, calm, loved, and completely safe. You have nothing to worry about from now on.

After you have brushed your teeth, combed your hair, and put on nice comfortable pajamas, it's time for you to snuggle down in bed and get ready for sleep. You can now pick any story to help you relax and drift off to an amazing sleep.

Make sure you listen to each story and follow along. Each story has a relaxing meditation to help you get cozy and comfortable for a good night's sleep.

Are you ready to begin your bedtime meditation stories? Choose any story to begin your adventure now!

CHAPTER 1

The Confident Mermaid Adventure

Hello and welcome.
I am so happy you are here to enjoy this guided meditation.
This bedtime story takes place on an island of paradise off Hawaii's coast, where the water is so pure and sparkles and shines with so much beauty.
Mythical mermaid people live here in the beautiful underwater kingdom.
You will meet a lovely princess mermaid.
She is a little shy but very friendly and kind.
My voice will guide you safely along a fantastic journey of confidence in these beautiful ocean waters of the Hawaiian Islands.
You will journey through coral reef gardens and will experience some incredible mermaid magic.

You and your mermaid princess friend will discover how to feel wonderfully confident and free to be your happiest selves as you settle in and begin this guided bedtime sleep meditation.

You may now gently close your eyes.

Start to imagine this exceptional, wonderful, and dreamy paradise in the tropical islands of Hawaii.

You are next to beautiful swaying palm trees and hibiscus flowers in a lush green jungle.

You can also see the most beautiful and bluest ocean you have ever seen.

Take a deep breath in and a long calm breath out.

Allow yourself to breathe a little more deeply now as you allow yourself to relax into this sleep meditation.

One of the islands in Hawaii contains a hidden cove.

This is a private beach with gorgeous white sands and a tiny little bay.

This place is secret from the outside world.

No tourists and no fishermen have ever been here before.

This is the magical, mystical cove of peace.

It is a safe haven for mermaid people to relax on dry land.

The waves gently flow onto the shore, and the ocean is shimmering in the moonlight.
You can see all of the stars and the galaxies from right here where you are standing.
There is a cool, refreshing breeze across the water and makes the palm trees rustle so softly.
You feel so amazing, grateful, and special to be here in this beautiful paradise.
You feel your body happily relax here as you just walk along the sand.
Dip your toes into the pure ocean water.
You have heard about the legend of mermaids and would very much like to meet one.
You then spot a beautiful spiral shell on the shore and hold it up to your ear.
You can hear the sound of the ocean from within the shell.
You start to make a special wish to see a real-life mermaid.

Suddenly glittering in the moonlight, a mermaid pops her head out of the water and swims onto shore not too far from you.
She has big green eyes with long shiny red hair.

She is decorated with beautiful seashell jewelry and has a smooth turquoise tail.
Wow, this is so amazing!
You are now filled with joy.
You walk closer slowly to meet this mermaid.
Mermaids can sometimes be very shy to humans.
She does seem a little shy as she just studies your face curiously.
It is as though she has never seen a human up close and personal before.
You give a gentle wave and smile.
You sit next to her in the sand and introduce yourself.
You explain that you are so happy to meet her.
She shyly introduces herself as Natasha, the mermaid princess.
Even though she is of royalty, she is still timid.
You explain to her that this is perfectly fine.
It is normal, and everyone feels shy from time to time, particularly when meeting new people or when in new situations.
Sometimes what can help is to sometimes pretend to feel more confident than you may actually feel inside.
You explain that everything in our life is a reflection of us, just like a mirror.
If we look scared and anxious and shy with our bodies, other people are more likely to reflect back

to us those same feelings, but if we take a deep breath and relax our bodies, smile, and love, we will look and feel confident and friendly.

Then people will reflect back to us happiness, kindness, friendliness, and love.

Natasha looks down in the water and sees her reflection looking back at her in the moonlight.

She smiles and seems surprised and happy when she sees her reflection also smiles back at her.

She asks if you would like to see where she lives.

You nod your head, and then she sprinkled some gold dust which magically gives you a mermaid tail.

Your tail is rainbow-colored with pinks, purples, and blues all blending in together so beautifully.

The scales on your tail sparkle and reflect all the different colors of the rainbow.

Wow it looks so magical and gorgeous.

Natasha then sprinkles some more gold dust onto you for you to be able to breathe underwater.

You feel so incredibly excited now as you follow Natasha.

She dives into the ocean, and you both go swimming so fast with your new tail.

You start diving and dipping joyfully through the clear and pure ocean water.

You are looking forward to meeting all the sea creatures and exploring her palace.

You both swim past a coral reef with dolphins, and you hold their fins and glide through the water.
You give a turtle a high five that swims past you.
Then you swim and play with a clownfish.
Then you start to see other mermaid people and Natasha talks to lots of people.
Wow she is so kind and so loveable.
Lots of sea creatures and mermaid people love her very much.

Natasha should never forget this when meeting new people or when she is in a new place with a different environment.
She is so liked and loved already, and this is definitely something to feel confident about.
She laughs and then thanks you so much for helping her to see this.
Sometimes everyone is so busy worrying about themselves that they probably don't notice they look shy.

You swim with Natasha some more through her beautiful underwater kingdom.

You swim past mermaids brushing their hair, and you see mermen working out with big shells.

You see merbabies just sleeping or playing around.

You see others reading ancient books about Atlantis, playing cards, and storytelling.

They are all too absorbed in their own lives to care about whether she looks shy or not.

Natasha laughs and thinks that she has been worried about things that are totally unnecessary for a long time.

You both laugh, and you both let go of the fear of what people may think of you.

You both now immediately look and feel so much more confident in yourselves.

Wow this is so wonderful.

You ask Natasha curiously what divine talents she has that she thinks are very special?

She tells you she loves to make beautiful jewelry.

She smiles so widely when you explain that this something to really be proud of and confident about.

You think to yourself of your very own unique talents too.

As you both swim through the beautiful coral gardens, Natasha tells you that sometimes she feels a lot of pressure to act like a princess.
This makes her very self-conscious at times.
You suggest to her to just be herself and love who she really is.
Then everyone will love her honesty and reflect it back to her.
Mermaid people are all different and wonderful in their own unique ways.
It is so exhausting and unnatural not to be yourself.
Just be who you are and let your light shine to the world.

You both laugh together now, and both let go of this idea that you're not allowed to be your authentic selves because in truth and reality, you have every permission to be your true selves now.
Everyone else is taken, so be yourself.
You both now immediately look more happy and relaxed.

It is okay to be quieter than other people.
You don't have to be the loudest person.
That is perfectly natural and normal because you may not want to be the center of attention all the time.
There is nothing to feel shy about as it is normal and healthy to be a quiet person.
You are just as wonderful, amazing, valuable, and interesting as those who have loud voices.
You can both be quietly confident because this is a beautiful and powerful thing.

Natasha swims around in a happy circle, smiles, and thanks you endlessly for your wise advice.
You also tell Natasha to look people in the eye when talking to them so you can really connect with them.
It gets easier the more you practice and makes you feel super confident.
Also, it is excellent manners to look people in the eyes when you are speaking with them.
She thanks you again for your wisdom.
In return, she gives you a massive white pearl that is round and glimmering beautifully in the crystal-clear ocean waters.
You are feeling so happy and confident now.

You swim around with your rainbow tail and stretch your arms out and take up as much space as you can.
I am confident.
Natasha laughs and does the same.
You both share your positive affirmations with each other, which helps you feel super confident.
I am safe.
I am smart.
I am loved.
I am healthy.
I am enough.
I am worthy.
I am important.
I can do anything.

A group of mermaids from another kingdom visits you both and swims up to you and Natasha.
They ask you both for directions to the palace.
You and Natasha both smile, look them in the eyes, and gesture with your arms to clearly point the way.
They all smile back at you and Natasha, and they thank you both and swim off in their way.
Natasha turns to you so happily.
She has now become so confident, and you feel even more confident now.

Just watching her apply everything you both have learned about feeling confident.
Awesome job and well done.

You may wish to celebrate her confidence and your confidence as well by swimming through the coral palace and through the pure ocean water with dolphins and fishes.
Enjoy the colorful coral garden palace and just love being in the beautiful and peaceful paradise.
Whatever your heart desires, you can now do it with confidence, happiness, and ease.
You are feeling so very special, joyful, and wonderful about the new possibilities in life.
You now have a friendly smile and a confident heart.
You accept and love who you truly are.
My voice is going to leave you soon to sleep deeply now.
Relax into the most peaceful and happiest sleepy dreams.
I wish you every ounce of happiness and love.
May you enjoy your blissful and sweet dreams.

CHAPTER 2

The Magic Carpet Ride

Hello and welcome to this guided, enchanted adventure story.

Very soon, you will love and enjoy having your very own magic carpet ride.

My voice will guide you happily and safely through this guided sleep meditation to a whole new wonderful world for you to relax and to use your wonderful imagination.

You will enjoy and take a magic carpet ride full of delight and make some fantastic new friends.

You will feel so free and happy.

Anything is possible when we choose a new point of view.

You can let go of negative thoughts and rise above them to be positive.

Life is so much more fun this way.

When we let go of negativity, the world is so exciting and such a magical place to see.

As you snuggle under the covers and get really cozy, you may close your eyes now and enjoy the darkness behind your eyelids.

You feel your body start to relax, and you feel little tingles of excitement as you feel that there is lots of magic in the air.

You know that something wonderful and amazing is about to happen.

Now take a deep breath in and out.

Feel so happy as you imagine what life could be like.

You can hear a slight rustle at your window.

You feel a rush of joy because you can see the most outstanding real-life magic carpet hovering and floating in the moonlight waiting just for you.

The moonlight is shining down with a safe and loving energy.

You step onto the magic carpet, and you are pleasantly surprised by how soft it feels under your bare feet.

You sit down and run your hands over the carpet's fluffy soft fabric.

It makes you feel warm and safe inside.
You can also see golden tassels hanging down from each corner of the carpet.
The magic carpet is woven from richly colorful Persian fabrics and has intricate designs.
You can see pictures from many legends and stories throughout history.
Wow how fascinating!
You sense that this is a very ancient and special magic carpet.
You feel so blessed to be riding on it.
As soon as you think this positive and grateful thought, the carpet lifts up and hovers in the air before taking off.
Now you are flying through the shimmering starlight.
Suddenly you find yourself on the carpet flying over the beautiful Arabian desert.

You can see the sand glittering a little in the moonlight.
You take a deep breath in and feel that there is so much space here.
It is so quiet and peaceful and really beautiful.

Now all of a sudden, the magic carpet ripples, which was seems to be excitement.
Then it rises about in the air.
Your carpet now catches a gust of wind and rushes up into the air.
Oh my!
This is so much fun!
Anything you wish is its command.
You feel a warm, calm breeze across your face and through your hair.
You rush through the night sky.
The happier and loved you feel, the more you appreciate and be grateful for what you see around you and in your heart, the faster the carpet flies and the higher it goes.
Wow this is so much fun.
You can now see a gorgeous palace shimmering in the starlight.
It has enormous impressive domed-shaped rooftops made of marble and gold.
It has beautiful wavy designs and looks like the desert sands inspired the design.
The palace is so beautiful.
You happily wish there were some friends to see and enjoy this with you and share this adventure.

As you and your magic carpet fly closer to the fantastic palace, you can see two people standing in front under a giant palm tree.
As you fly closer, you can see it is a girl and a boy.
They are smiling up at you and waving.
You sense that they are good kind people.
The carpet flies down and hovers in front of them.
The boy and the girl both look very familiar to you.
It is as though maybe you have seen them somewhere else before.
You introduce yourself, and you meet Jasmine.
She is a kind-hearted and intelligent young Arabian princess.
She has lovely dark and long hair.
She climbs onto your magic carpet, and then you meet a funny and clever Arabian prince who tells you his name is Ali.
He then happily climbs onto the carpet to ride with you as well.
As the three of you ride together and fly up on your magic carpet, Princess Jasmine gives you a wonderful and royal tour of the palace in the sky.

She points out the gardens, the pools, and the gorgeous buildings from the sky above as you fly.

Then a city of fantastic architecture appears in the distance.

The three of you look down and admire the stunning art and unique swirls and spirals of so many beautiful colors.

You can see reds, purples, blues, turquoise, and greens.

These colorful designs are celebrating the artistic culture of the Persian empire throughout history.

Wow.

What a magnificent and wonderful city this is.

As you three continue to fly over the desert land and above huge sand dunes, Ali tells jokes and makes you all laugh.

As you laugh, you look up, and you can see the stars shimmering and twinkling in the sky.

You can see the stars so clearly, and they look so incredible.

There are many more stars in the universe than grains of sand on Earth, Jasmine said.

The whole sky is shimmering with the glorious starlight.

You point up at shooting star beaming across the sky.

You all cheer with excitement.
Wow you feel so happy.
You now promise to let go of all negativity and always choose positive thoughts and positive feelings because then your life can be like a magical adventure.

You are just enjoying the calm, cool breeze flying through the night sky on your magic carpet with your fun and amazing new friends.
Suddenly a beautiful sight appears before you.
You see a desert oasis of aqua blue pools of water.
It looks like a glowing jewel in the desert sands.

This peaceful and beautifully lush Oasis looks like a mystical and enchanting mirage.
As you get closer, you can see it is real.
Wow it is so breathtakingly beautiful.
This is truly amazing.

You can see friendly camels drinking at the water's edge of the Oasis.
Then look up and start smiling at you all with their big funny teeth and gummy smiles.
You have never ridden a camel before.
Maybe now is the time.
It is entirely up to you.

You can go anywhere on your magic carpet with your new friends.
You can ride across the middle east, Africa, Asia, Europe, or even Oceania.
You can travel anywhere your heart desires.
You can go to a whole new world of possibilities of shining and sparkling dreams.
You can create the most positive and amazing ideas and exploring the wonderful world on your magic carpet.
You feel so blissfully happy and peacefully powerful because you now know that you can create positive thoughts instantly.
You can make the most beautiful things into reality and experiences for yourself and others.

You can choose to think positive thoughts which keep you soaring high and moving forward fast both on your magic carpet and in your life.

Now our adventure is starting to end.
I want you to always keep riding high, thinking positively, and having fun on your enchanted journey.
I want you to keep having fun on your magic carpet ride for as long as you wish in your happiest and dreamiest sleep.
I wish you all the happiness in the world and good night.

CHAPTER 3

The Fairy Forest

Welcome children to experience your imagination and happiness where we will focus only on feeling good.
Are you ready for this adventure?
Close your eyes now and make yourself really comfortable.
Stretch your whole body out and let your arms, legs, and belly relax.

Take a big deep breath in through your nose and slowly and gently breathe out through your mouth. Again take a deep breath in through your nose and slowly and gently breathe out through your mouth.

One more time, deep breath in through your nose and slowly and gently breathe out through your mouth.

Amazing.

You're doing fantastic.

Now imagine that you are walking along fresh green soft grass with your bare feet.

The grass is cool, refreshing, soft, and a little ticklish under your feet.

You feel so calm and so relaxed.

This is called grounding.

This keeps your energy planted in the ground, and you feel connected to the earth and to all of nature.

Our planet earth has an amazing and very special energy, and you are now connected to it.

Now imagine looking up into the night sky and seeing the beautiful stars sparkling across the sky.

You notice that one star is a bit brighter than all of the others.

It is shining the brightest out of all of them.

You can see it twinkling as it shines its light down onto you.

Suddenly a huge beam of light shines down from the star around your whole body.

This is such a beautiful silvery-white light that is glowing all around you.

You are now shining like the brightest star.

This starlight is made out of pure love and is keeping you safe and happy.

This light is always around you.

You feel so relaxed and peaceful.

Amazing.

You are doing so great.

Now imagine you're standing at the edge of the enchanted forest in the starlight.

You can see a path glistening between the trees shining down and invites you to walk along and follow it.

You step along this magical path made up of green grass that is so soft under your feet.

You feel very safe and happy here in this ancient forest.

You have a feeling and sense that the trees here are wise and old and friendly.

Here there are lots of lovely animals waiting to meet you.

You look around you and see that the trees have what looks like faces in their ancient trunks.

They all look they are smiling at you so friendly.

Suddenly a fairy flies by your face and starts to just hover in front of you.

Wow it's a real-life fairy!

Their wings look so delicate like a butterfly, and it has a golden glow around itself.

It smiles with you with such a kind smile and then darts off further into the forest.

As you follow this twisting and turning path, you admire the huge colorful flowers growing extra big and beautiful because the forest is enchanted with glorious vines.
The vines have flowers hanging down along the pathway.
The plants and trees seem to just be sparkling.
As you look closer, you realize that there are glow worms and fireflies and fairy lights shimmering everywhere.
This forest is just so pure, and you feel so safe, happy, and loved here.

You now can hear faint sounds of enchanting music drifting through the beautiful forest trees.
You follow the sound of music and the path as you come to a clearing.
In front of you is the most gorgeous scenery.
There is a perfect circle of soft green grass glowing silver in the moonlight with mushrooms and red-spotted toadstools forming a circle in the grass.

The fairies are in a circle smiling and waving to you and welcoming you into their clearing.
You see elves playing bagpipes, flutes, fiddles, and harps, creating some magical music.
Now the fairies and pixies are all dancing and fluttering in between trees and toadstools.
They all wave at you and invite you to join them.
You dance and twirl with them in the soft grass.
Wow this is so much fun!
You feel so free as you laugh about and dance to the mystical happy music.
You now have some time to just enjoy yourself in the secret enchanted part with your new fairy, elf, and pixie friends.

The moon is high in the sky shining, and the magical music starts to fade away as the elves, pixies, and fairies dance off into the forest.
You sense that it is time to leave the clearing.
You are feeling so joyful, peaceful, and alive.
You walk back along the moonlit path on the soft green grass back through the big wise old trees.
Past the gorgeous flowers.
Fairies are sitting on the flowers and smile at you and wave goodbye.

As you walk past, two glowing fairies fly and hover in front of you.
They smile at you with delight, wave, and dart off into the forest.
You follow the path back the way you came twisting and turning through the Enchanted forest.
You feel so safe and loved in the pure moonshine.
You are so relaxed as you take one step after another, walking slowly between the trees.

Your whole body feels heavy and peaceful.
You notice how quiet and still the forest has become.
All of the creatures have now gone to sleep.
You see fairies sleeping in the beautiful flowers.
You also see them sleeping under the giant mushrooms and sleeping in the tree houses.
Everything is so calm and peaceful as the forest falls fast asleep.
You walk to the edges of the trees and then straight into the bed where you sleep all snug and cozy under the covers.
Your whole body is calm and heavy and relaxed.
You feel so special and so happy.

You know you can visit the enchanted forest anytime you wish.
Sweet dreams.

CHAPTER 4

Rapunzel and Believing

Once upon a time, in a dreamy land far, far away, there is a long blonde-haired girl in a tower with no stairway.
This girl is named Rapunzel, and her hair is like gold. She is trapped by an evil spell by someone cold and jealous.
Tonight you will visit Rapunzel and help her realize something that can only be discovered with a happy heart and a mind that is wise.
When we believe in ourselves we can do anything and find within ourselves the answers to be free from everything.
Welcome to this lovely enchanted sleep-guided meditation story.
It will lead you to your happiest and most wonderful relaxation.

We will journey safely together into this land of magical dreams.

My voice will guide you gently to this land across rainbows and moonlight beams.

Are you ready to meet Rapunzel and enjoy this beautiful fairytale story?

As you help the princess, you will also discover your own glory and improve your self-beliefs.

Close your eyes now and gently take a big deep breath in and out.

You're doing fantastic.

Your muscles are starting to relax and unwind.

Now breathe in a little more deeply and settle in peacefully with ease to this guided sleep meditation story.

Now you can easily picture the moonlight glittering down through your window surrounding your whole body in the pure energy of love and safety.

It is such a gorgeous silvery glow.

Your heart swells up with happiness as the beams of light sparkle down, and the rainbow appears in the nighttime sky.

This colorful enchanted night rainbow will transport you safely to the land of fairy tales.

You find yourself relaxing more as the light of the rainbow surrounds you allowing your thoughts to drift.

Images start appearing but not too fast and not too slow.

It is just right for you.

Simply relax as my voice drifts along the rainbow with you.

You drift along with it through the glittering night rainbow into the land of dreams and fairy tales.

You now happily find yourself at the other end of the rainbow in an open flower field of daisies.

Snowcapped mountains of pine trees surround you.

You look around you, and you cannot see anyone else or any buildings here as far as your eyes can see.

The air is so fresh and healthy here.

The air is a little cool, but the sun on your skin feels warm.

Take a deep breath in and enjoy the lovely fragrance of flowers and fresh Jasmine and lavender around you.

You can see bumblebees just buzzing lazily around the flowers of tulips and daisies.

You admire what a beautiful place this is.

This meadow has an energy that is so pure and clean, and healthy.

You run through the meadow with your arms outstretched and twirl around so freely.

You grab some daises and wear them in your hair.

Now while you are enjoying this, you hear a lovely voice singing an old song drifting through the mountain air.

You notice the beautiful singing seems to be coming from behind some trees.

You now notice there is a tower standing all by itself.

As you begin to walk closer, you can see the tower has a fairytale-style room at the top.

There is a pointer on top of the tower to reflect the sun, and seems to sparkle with like a magical light.

How interesting.

You walk around the tower and notice a beautiful ivy vine growing around the outside.

There doesn't appear to be a door either.

How strange.

The lovely singing is much louder now.

You can see the window at the top of the tower starts to open, and the gentle singing stops.

A beautiful face looks down at you from the window.

The girl in the tower just looks at you and studies you curiously.

Then she smiles happily and gives you a friendly wave.

You instantly feel that you will get along really well and become friends.

You realize this must be Rapunzel.

She happily lets her hair down for you to climb up the tower and meet her enormous silky golden blonde hair.

It looks like golden strands all spun together and is cascading down to where you are standing on the meadow ground below.

You easily climb up her braided hair, which feels like a smooth golden rope glowing in the sun all the way into the window.

At the top of the tower, you can see the meadow, valleys, and mountains.

The view from up here is breathtaking.

Although the tower feels really small with just one room with a bed, a harp, and a bookcase of old fairy tales.

There is also a teeny tiny room to the side of the tower, which is a dressing room for the princess to sit and brush her hair.

She tells you that she passes the time by singing and playing with the beautiful and cheery birds which comes to visit her at her window sill.

You ask Rapunzel why she feels trapped here.

She tells you an evil person casted a spell on her, and there doesn't appear to be a way out for her.

Rapunzel tells you sadly that a lovely prince used to visit her but was not able to save her.

You ask Rapunzel why she doesn't break the spell and save herself.

Maybe she just feels more trapped than she actually is.

There must be a way out.

She looks at you with wide-eyed amazement because she has never thought of this before.

You suggest and explain to Rapunzel that the only power a person has over you is what you allow to be true.

What if you're only ever trapped in your own mind and that anything and everything is actually possible.

There is a solution for everything, and the answers are always within us if we just calm our minds, listen to our hearts, and believe in ourselves.

With amazement and excitement, Rapunzel nods her head happily and agrees with you wholeheartedly.

She understands now that all she has to do is believe in herself and trust her heart.

This spell won't hold any power over her.

All that really matters is the surprise and realization that she starts to think about her freedom.

Then a friendly and cheerful bluebird flies in and rests on the window sill carrying a stick from the pine trees in its beak.

Rapunzel looks at the bluebird, then looks at you, and her eyes light up with joy.

She just came up with a brilliant idea.

Rapunzel unravels her glorious hair and tells you to climb back down that tower.

So you climb all the way down her golden hair and step down gently into the meadow.

As you look up, you watch her escape plan unfold.

Rapunzel grabs the stick from the bluebird and jams it into the window's hinges, creating what looks like a hook.

She ties the end of her hair around the stick and then, with a confident grin, climbs down her hair.

She is working her way down from the top of the tower to the bottom.

Wow Rapunzel is saving herself!

She scales down the tower quickly, happily, and cheerfully.

She loves her newfound confidence and self-belief.

When she reaches the meadow ground, she gives her hair a good yank, and the rest of her hair falls into the meadow.

You are surprised to see Rapunzel rolling around in the grass, laughing with happiness and joy.

She actually freed herself.

You can't help but laugh as well.

It feels so good to laugh as you realize how important and easy it is to believe in ourselves.

Rapunzel finds it so funny that the answer was there all along with her.

The so-called spell was only something she was allowing to be true.

She had the power to break it the whole time.

All she had to do was believe in herself and know that positive energy and our inner spirit are always more powerful.

Just be watching Rapunzel learning this lesson with her makes your confidence rise.

You think to yourself how great it feels to laugh about it as you feel your confidence raised.

You believe in yourself more now too.

Any previously held fears feel like distant memories that now mean nothing.

Rapunzel runs through the field of daisies and tulips with her arms outstretched.

You run through the field with her as you both twirl around and announce to the world that from now on, you will write your own stories and live your happiest, fullest and freest life, sing, have a voice to share with the world, and to share all of your unique talents to the world.

Rapunzel thanks you endlessly for helping her to realize the truth.

Do you feel even more inspired to do the same in your own life?

To believe in yourself and live freely and joyfully?

Trusting that there are always happy solutions in any situation.

When we believe in ourselves and in our own power within anything is possible.

What a fantastic adventure you're having in the land of dreams and fairy tales.

Learning to believe in yourself just like how Rapunzel did.

You are feeling so wonderfully happy and also sleepy and tired.

It has been a very big day, and you are not sure if this is all a dream.

You may wish to keep exploring the beautiful relaxing nature around you of the flower meadow and the snow-capped mountains with your friend Rapunzel.

Your whole body has drifted deeper and deeper now into this guided meditation.

You are in a beautiful dreamland now as you switch off and go with the flow to my voice to your most relaxing and blissful sleep.

My voice will leave you soon because you are loving drifting into your happiest and most confident and peaceful dreams now.

Knowing now that you believe in yourself that you can be and do anything.

As my voice fades away, you are feeling so happy, loved, cozy and confident.

Since you believe in yourself, you now know that you can explore your happiest fairytale dream adventures anytime you wish.

Sweet Dreams.

CHAPTER 5

The Sleepy Animal Kingdom

Gently close your eyes and stretch out your body.
Make sure you are in a completely comfortable position, so you can relax and start to dream.
The wonderful meditation magic can happen when you are almost asleep.
Take a deep breath in and a calm breath out.
One more time, take a deep breath in and a long calm breath out.
That's wonderful.
It is so exciting that the animals have invited you to play with them tonight.
As you start to relax more and more, imagine the starlight streaming in through your window.
Now, imagine this glorious starlight surrounding your whole body.

This divine light is the energy of pure love and it always keeps you safe.

To your surprise and amazement, you start to see grass growing on the floor.
Plants are sprouting up out of nowhere.
Your cupboard becomes a huge tree.
The light becomes a full moon.
Vines start to hang down from the ceiling.
Your room disappears around you and green leaves start to grow.
Exotic flowers start to bloom and the most beautiful tropical plants you have ever seen start to appear everywhere.

You notice that your bed is no longer a bed but it is now a soft patch of spotted mushrooms.

A sloth swings down from a branch and winks at you.
You instantly realize you are now in a sleepy jungle.
The moonlight shines down through the trees bathing the sleepy jungle in the silvery light of love.

You look around and you see that everything glows in the moonshine and looks magical.
With your bare feet, you step onto the soft fluffy grass.
You instantly feel safe and connected to the Earth here.

A feeling and sense of fun starts to dance within your heart.
This is your special adventure!

What animals do you want to meet tonight?
A monkey with a huge grin and a long curly tail swings over to you and waves you to climb up the vine.
You discover you can climb so easily just like a monkey.
You start to swing through the trees with your new monkey friend.
You can feel the fresh night breeze on your face.
As you catch and swing from the vines, you feel so free.
You spot some gorillas on the jungle floor relaxing next to very big plants.

These friendly gorillas smile to you and you climb down to meet them.
They show you how to walk like a gorilla on your knuckles and teach you how to be proud of yourself.
They show you how to peel bananas in the best way possible.

Now you see some eyes looking at you through the plants.
A black panther appears between the leaves and walks towards you.

The panther has a beautiful black coat.
It is glistening in the moonlight.
The panther nods at you and invites you to climb on its back.

You hop on and pet its smooth fur.

It starts running through the trees.

The panther is running so fast.

Running past huge exotic flowers and plants.
You feel so happy and light as you race through the jungle on your super-fast panther friend.

The sleepy jungle has the friendliest animals in the world.
They are so happy here and they live in perfect harmony with each other.
You start to hear the sound of flowing water.

Now, you see a jungle stream of crystal-clear water.
Your panther friend stops by the stream and you hop off and pet its soft black coat.
You look at the water sparkling in the moonlight as it bubbles along and into a pond.

There are huge gorgeous lily pads with pink flowers and big green frogs sitting on them in this huge pond.

The frog smiles up at you and invites you onto its lily pad.
You step onto the green pad and from one lily pad to another across the water.
Wow this is so amazing!

You are as light as a feather and can jump far like a frog, hopping over lily pads.

A brightly colored toucan flies down from a nearby tree and gestures you to follow it.

You look up at the toucan's big beak and dazzling tropical feathers.
You think wow such an incredible bird.

You let the toucan guide you the rest of the way.
As you walk along the green soft fluffy grass, it flies just above you, so you know where to go through the sleepy forest.

You feel that it is taking you through this sleepy jungle to a very special place.

Now, you arrive at the coziest, dreamiest, and sleepiest place in the sleepy jungle.
You have arrived at a sleeping cave of a tiger.

This is a safe, dark, and secret cave.
It is hidden between the sleeping sloths.

You crawl quietly inside the cave and you see colors of orange and black.

You see a striped tiger relaxing happily in the cave.
You lie down next to its soft, warm body.
It is breathing slowly and heavily in

And out.

In

And out.

You feel so safe and so calm.

Resting next to this big friendly tiger are two birds laying down near you with their wings folded.
You can see out of the cave entrance to the nearby branches are sloths sleeping lazily in the trees above.

The entire jungle now starts to rest.
The moon hides behind some clouds and seems like it is sleeping too.
Your eyes now feel very heavy and your breathing gets deeper and deeper.
You close your eyes.

You feel so cozy and warm and special.
You feel yourself drifting off.

Into your happiest dreams.

As you sleep deeply now in the tiger's sleeping cave in the sleepy jungle, you feel so happy and so blessed.
You know you are so safe here and so loved by all the jungle animals around you as you sleep even more deeply now.

With pure peace in your heart, you know that you are so very special.

You feel so wonderful exactly as you are.
Your animal friends of the sleepy jungle are waiting just for you.

You can visit any time you wish.

Sleepy jungle dreams.

Have you ever met a lion before?
A real lion in the wild?
Well, lions get up at night when all of the other animals in the savanna start to sleep at night.

Tonight Leo the magnificent lion king and Leon his fun and playful cub, are inviting you to roam about freely with them.
Joining them as they like to explore and have the dreamiest and the most wonderful nighttime adventure that you can possibly imagine, before you drift off to sleep.

Now, as you snuggle in and start to feel cozy and comfortable, you can close your eyes and show your lion friends how you are.

So very quiet and being totally still.

These sleepy lions always know what is going on around them by listening carefully to the sounds of the breeze and remaining so very still.

They pay attention with all of their lion senses because even when lions look like they're lazing about so happily, maybe even seeming to be sound asleep.

Don't be fooled.

Those sleepy lions are always ready to pounce and prowl and maybe even roar.

Sometimes even just for fun to surprise other sleepy animals around them.

It is also to remind everyone who really is king of the sleepy savanna.

I think you are going to enjoy and be surprise tonight on your very own marvelous dream adventure.

You may feel very excited inside and even might find yourself starting to dream away.

Dreaming of wide green open plains.

You see with your mind's eye, the tall and strong baobab trees.

You see so many interesting and wonderful rock formations.

You can also easily see the bright and clear moon.
It is high in the sky and everything glowing in the moonshine is enchanted by a silvery moonlight that sparkles beautifully.
You now hear all the peaceful calming sounds of this place including the soft running water from a gentle stream.

You now peer through the clear moonlight.
You see two amazing animals drinking water from the stream.
One of them runs over to you and how you can make out a young lion's face.

It is a lion with friendly eyes and a mischievous grin.
This young lion introduces himself as Leon.
Now his father Leo walks over to you looking proud.
He has a majestic mane that looks like a rock star.
He has such a great proud posture.

Leo holds out his massive paw for you to shake as he tells you his name.

He is king Leo the pride of the land.

King Leo and Leon smiles warmly at you and you instantly sense they are kindhearted.

You feel so safe and calm in their presence because you know they will protect you no matter what.

You feel like a soft tickly feeling from the lion fur of Leon as he nuzzles playfully into you.

He has a warm fuzzy coat.

King Leo tells you they are going to take you on a night tour of the pride lands.

It is to do night watching of the sleeping animals because they are the protectors of the sleepy savannah.

They would love for you to see some of the most fun places.

You feel so excited now.

You begin to follow the path of the stream.

With Leo prancing ahead you and Leon are hopping, skipping, tripping and jumping along.

As you follow the long relaxing flowing stream, you see it winds out to a clear open of the grassland.

Now you see before you this beautiful savannah.

It stretches out so wide and far.
You see the lovely clear water of the stream which flows into a pond.
This pond has become quite muddy and all of a sudden, you hear the funny sounds of loud snoring. You can't quite make out where it's coming from, but you see a huge rock stuck in the mud there.

This rock suddenly moves, and you see a humongous muddy face and you realize it is a massive hippopotamus.
It is resting, snoring, and happily sleeping.

The giant sleepy hippo rolls over with an enormous snore coming from its huge nostrils.
Leo grins and very soon, he tickles the hippo's nose with a feather and the hippo blows out an even bigger snore.
It was the loudest and funniest snore you have ever heard.

The hippos wriggles a bit deeper into the mud.

Leon dips his little lion head into the goopy brown mud.
He suddenly presses his paw onto your hand.
You feel so wild and free like a lion.

You feel that you truly belong in this lion pride now.

Now having checked on the hippos, you all race out across the open grassland.
You run as fast as you possibly can, but you are no match for King Leo.
He is the fastest lion in all of the sleepy savannah.

King Leo is helping you out because you are now a part of the pride.
The king of the lions bows his strong neck down and lets you climb onto his back.

You now hold on very tight to King Leo's big Rockstar mane and fluffy fur.
He runs faster and faster with Leon running as fast alongside him.

You all race through the savannah.

You leap over many rocks and now are darting through the trees.
Everything around you becomes a blur.

After a little while, you all slow down again.
You slow down to a gentle walking pace feeling so relaxed.

The three of you arrive at the beautiful tall trees where all of the sleeping giraffes like to lay about as they rest.
Underneath the green leafy trees, you see all the giraffes peacefully curled up on the ground.

They have long necks curved around and relaxed.

They are resting so easily on their long front legs.
Every giraffe is smiling happily as you see each one snooze.
The giraffes look so funny because they are twisting their necks into strange sleeping positions.
Everyone appears to be calm and cozy.
You are sleeping so well and enjoying all of this fun relaxing happy time.
You start to notice King Leo is so powerful, proud, and compassionate.
Here you see and know that he has great respect for this circle of life.

Each and every night, he chooses to check in on his sleeping kingdom.

He makes sure they are sleeping so safe and soundly.
Feeling so blissfully protected as they sleep.

You now see and understand Leon loves learning from his father and likes to have fun along the way.
As you continue to explore more, you will be surprised to discover that the lions watch over the entire circle of life every night.
They watch over the sleepy elephants to the sleeping eagles.
From the relaxing meer cats to all of the sleeping zebras.
Every animal in the sleepy savannah are all looked after by the protective King Leo.

Now this sleepy restful night adventure is all done now.
You feel such amazing joy in your heart.
You feel so happy and will have such an incredible sleep.
It is so fun and free to be a part of the lion's pride.
Together you are all traveling all the way back over the soft sleepy grasslands.

You go all the way back to the biggest rock in the savannah.

You see he has a lovely cozy and calming cave.
Here inside is the safest cave.
This is where you find the mama lion, Leon's brothers and sisters and the rest of the lion pride.
They are all now sleeping.
You are so curious but you are becoming more tired than before.
You crawl into the smooth sleepy cave with all the sleepy lions.
You lie down to sleep in the safest, softest and warmest space just for you.
This lovely cave is so dark and so cozy.
It feels so warm and safe sleeping with the wonderful pride of the lions.
You are all nestled together for a deep deep sleep.
You feel the soft fur of the sleeping lions and you feel completely safe.
You easily fall asleep.

You feel so protected and at home.
You are among the friendliest of all the lions.
You are the most special new member of the sleepy lion's pride.
Now as you relax more and more.
You continue to sleep and all you hear are the lions snoozing and relaxing.

They are so happy together.
You all enjoy a healthy restful sleep at night.

Your entire body relaxes and you sink down into a deep sleep.
You enjoy all of your positive lovely dreams of the sleepy savannah.
You continue to feel so extremely happy inside.
You wish your sweetest, coziest, and happiest lion dreams to appear.
Now the meditation adventure of the sleepy safari begins.

All you need to do is relax your body and allow your imagination to take you on the most wonderful places.
You are on a very special sleepy safari.
It is leaving you soon and you better get ready.

You close your eyes and you make sure they are very comfortable.
As you settle in, you may think about which animals you wish to see.

You take a deep breath in and a calm breath out.
Again you take a deep breath in and a long calm breath out.

You continue to breathe and you start to feel more and more relaxed.

Amazing! Your body feels all heavy and floppy now.

Now imagine you are standing on an African savannah.
Imagine there are sleepy planes all around you and as far as you can see.
The orange sun is shining brightly.
The earth feels warm under your bare feet.
You feel yourself connecting to the land here.
You are very excited and you are here for a sleepy safari.

You suddenly see a jeep cruiser driving towards you. It is in a cloud of dust and you can see the color of the jeep as it gets closer and closer.

You realize it is my tour guide.

It is coming to pick you up for your safari adventure. The big car comes to a halt with dust swirling everywhere.

When you see who is driving it, you are very surprised.

There is a tiger behind the wheel with a safari hat.

He is wearing a Hawaiian shirt with binoculars around his neck.

He gives you a friendly smile and waves his paw to you.

He checks his clipboard and reads your name out loud.

You smile and say yes.

The tiger leans over and pushes the door open for you to climb inside.

Your tiger guide drives you super fast across the sleepy safari.

He is a casual tiger and very easy going.

He has lots of fun.

This is no ordinary safari.

He drives you up a big grassy hill and you wonder where is he leading you?
There seems to be nothing around.
Now you see over the rise from the top of the hill is the most amazing scene in front of you.

There is a beautiful valley below with a river winding along and into a big blue pond.
Huge baobab trees dodge the landscape holding water in their bulging trunks.
There are grasslands and also a green forest area that is waiting for you to explore it.
You feel so peaceful here.
It is already lots of fun to be here in Africa.
Your tiger tour guide grins at you and looks pretty impressed with himself.
He tells you that this is the secret reserve.
That only the animals know about.
You feel so lucky to be here.
There are two friendly elephants greeting you at the top of the hill.
One for you and one for the tiger.

You climb onto your new elephant friend.
You hold onto the tufted hair on its back.
Your body wobbles and jiggles all over the place.
The elephant takes huge steps and walks slowly down the hill slope.
You are now down in the valley.
You climb off your elephant.

You feel very excited and very relaxed.
All of your favorite animals were right here in their natural habitat.
This is now your special time to meet the animals.
This is your very own sleepy safari, and your tiger tour guide is right here with you.
You can go running with the cheetahs or you may wish to go swimming on vines with the monkeys.
You could climb up trees and help the tall giraffes find the very best leaves.
You can visit the hippopotamus in its muddy waterhole.
There are meer cats, zebras, gazelles and every animal you wish to see.
You have some time now to explore the valley.
You meet all the animals your heart desires.

You are starting to feel even more sleepy and ready to be in your happiest dreams.

After having so much fun with the animals, you notice the sun is setting far in the distance.

It is glowing orange and fading now.

It dips below the horizon, and moonlight is shining over the valley.

The stars have come out to play.

They twinkle so beautifully in the night sky.

There are so many stars and you see them so clearly as you gaze up in awe.

You start to feel very very sleepy.

As the stars sparkle above you, the valley starts to fade.

As you get sleepier and sleepier, it is now time to return home to bed.

You wave goodbye to the animals of the secret valley.

You wave goodbye to your tiger tour guide.

He waves his paw to you and smiles.

You can now feel that you were in a warm cozy bed.

As you sleep deeply, now there is pure joy in your heart.

You know that anything is possible.

You are so very special and completely loved.
You can dream so happy now.
The animals can't wait for you to visit them again for another meditation adventure anytime you wish.
The sweet sleepy safari.

As you settle into the most comfortable and cozy position, you gently close your eyes.
Can you imagine a very special place?
The most wonderful fun tropical jungle where all of the animals live happily in harmony with each other.
I will let you on a very little-known secret.
There is such a place called a mindful jungle hidden deep within the calming valley.
It is between peaceful mountains where the animals gather together and meditate before falling deep asleep.
They drift into the most amazing dreams.
They fall asleep so fast and so well.
All these animals always wake up feeling so refreshed before having the most fun and delightful days.
They have focused positive minds because all of your favorite animals love to do their mindful sleep meditation.

They gather together under the trees.
They are inviting you to join them right now.
It feels very enchanting because the sun has already set and the stars have come out to twinkle in the night sky.
Everyone is feeling very sleepy and ready for a cozy sleep.
You feel so lucky to be invited.

The fluffy lion begins by taking three deep breaths in and out.
The lions can only do their mighty roars with very good deep breathing.
Together you breathe in and out.
You breathe deeply, just like the gentle breeze of the jungle trees.
You are doing fantastic!
You notice the lion is very tired and his breaths became big yawns.
You can't help but to do a mighty lion yawn as well.
The next elephant relaxes his heavy body from its elephant ears all the way down to its trunk and jaw, even all the way down to its feet.
Together you relax your whole body.
You feel all heavy and sleepy like your elephant friend.

Now the elephant yawns an even bigger yawn.

You all yawn too.

This is the biggest yawn you have ever yawned before.

Now a cute monkey calms its monkey mind.

Like the adorable monkey, you observe your thoughts before letting them float away like clouds in a night sky.

The monkey snuggles into a cozy position feeling sleepier and sleepier.

It is so very relaxing.

It does a little monkey yawn and ready to dream about the funniest things.

Together just like your monkey friend, you relax your body even more ready to dream about the most wonderful things that you can imagine.

You may notice the gentle giraffe practices patience very well listening high up to the sounds of the leaves rustling in the treetops and all of the noises in the distance.

Together you tune your ears noticing many different sounds both near and far far away.

You can hear the sound of your breathing.

Perhaps you are already asleep, and the cuddly bear notices its feelings.

Deep inside with all of its bare heart and all of its many feelings are welcome here.

Together you notice your feelings inside too.
As you breathe deeply and just observe them in your heart, the bear always feels warm and fuzzy inside.
Do you?

You feel so special to be here with your animal friends.
They are all so very friendly, kind hearted and snoozy.
Next, the furry fox stops fighting his foxy ways and wisely realizes it is enough exactly as it is.
Together you feel the wisdom inside you that you are enough and perfect exactly as you are.
You let go into a deep sleep.
Your mind switches off and you are almost dreaming away with delight.
Now the soothing squirrel stops squirreling about and becomes very still.
You notice the squirrel's breathing is slower because the squirrel is calm.

You are trusting that there is plenty of everything for everyone.

You relax even more and feel this sense of trust.

There are really no limits and there is so much abundance for all of us.

You start to become still because you are so comfortable here in your perfect sleeping position.

You are on the soft fluffy grass for the night.

Here under the trees is the happiest hedgehog that understands we are all different and that is okay.

It is wonderful.

The hedgehog relaxes its spine to be so friendly and kind.

It is no longer judging itself or judging the animals in the jungle.

They are now accepting them for who they are.

You send love and kindness to yourself and others.

You feel so nice and soft as you melt into a deep sleep.

When you finally stop sleeping and snoozing and dreaming all through the night, you will wake up just like a radiant rabbit tomorrow morning.

You will see the world with fresh eyes because tomorrow is a new day.

Just like the rabbit, you will feel ready to hop about.

You are feeling so calm, confident, and happy inside.

Now the moon is high in the sky above the sleepy jungle.

You know that you are safe and loved here among your animal friends.
Perhaps you are drifting deeper and deeper now into your lovely dreams.
You are loving this beautiful deep sleep here in the calming valley between the peaceful mountains.

Every part of you is now enjoying your deepest and loveliest sleep and it feels brilliant to be a wonderful human being which you already are.
You will snooze and sleep to your heart's content all through the night.

CHAPTER 6

The Magic Unicorn Adventure

Lay down and be still and quiet and peaceful in your bed while you listen.
You can close your eyes if you want to and use your imagination so you can see the story in your mind.
Make sure that everything is comfortable and that you are ready to relax.
A group of three dogs named Bella, Lucy and Jake were on a very special steam train.
They were going on a trip to the seaside.
This train ride was going to take quite a long time.
The dogs thought it was awesome that they were on this magical train.
It made lots of cool sounds as it chugged and chugged along.
It was the best train ever.

The only problem with this train was that it was full. There were no seats to be found anywhere.

The dogs had walked almost halfway through the train and they still couldn't find anywhere to sit.

They came across a cabin which had a very big unicorn standing in the front of the door.

This cabin could not allow dogs inside.

Lucy looked up and said, "hello um would it be alright if me and my sisters can go and sit in there with the unicorns? We can't find anywhere else to sit and this train is full. It would be nice if we can go and sit there."

The giant unicorn just stared down at Lucy and didn't change his face.

He didn't speak, smile or do anything.

Bella said, "he kind of reminds me of one of those guards that stands in front of the palace in London."

Jake says, "oh yeah. You're right he does look kind of intimidating. Do you think he understands us?"

A unicorn inside of the cabin had come to the window.

He slid the door open and said it's okay they can come in and sit with me.

The dogs looked up at the big giant scary looking unicorn who didn't make a single facial expression.

They decided to very slowly and carefully walk around him to get inside the cabin.

When they got inside, the unicorn that had already closed the door sat down on a very comfortable looking pillow.

In fact, the whole cabin was filled with soft plush pillows and blankets.

It looked very comfortable and inviting.

The unicorn introduced himself.

His name is Jack.

He is a prince.

He is very happy to meet you.

The dogs think it is very nice and thinks that it is kind of fancy.

Are you sure you are alright sitting here with us?

I feel like we have to be a royal or something to be sitting next to you.

The unicorn laughed and said, "you don't have to be a royal to be with me. You're very welcome to be next to me. I'm only a prince. That doesn't mean I'm not normal or anything. Does anyone want a chip?"

The prince takes out a bag of chips from his big suitcase and offered the dogs some chips.

When Bella opened the bag of chips a paper snake shot out and scared all the dogs.

They all jumped a little.

The prince thought that it was absolutely hilarious, and he was rolling across from them laughing and holding his stomach.

He thought it was so funny.

The dogs were already getting the idea that this prince was quite funny and had a sense of humor.

The dogs and the prince talked for a while on the train.

They introduced themselves and finding who they were and all about each other.

Unicorns are supposed to have wings, but the prince says he is not old enough to have wings.

His sister Selena has wings and she is a princess.

She is older than I am and better at everything than me.

She is like perfect.

She is kind.

She is sweet.

Jake asked the prince why he is on the train.

Does he have somewhere he needs to go?

The prince is actually on his way home.

He lives in a very special place.

He has been away at boarding school in the city and it is not time for him to go home.

What is boarding school?

Well it is a school where you stay and live there for a while.

Since he is a prince, he has to learn lots of fancy things like how to use the proper fork at the dinner table, how to behave at gatherings, how to speak and how to sit.

The prince said a lot of it is boring and it would be much more fun if he could just learn what you wanted to learn at school rather than learn what everyone else tells you.

Maybe the prince would actually like school but now it is just plain and too boring for him.

He is glad he is going home.

Where does he exactly live?

Through the window of the train came a bright light.

It was the brightest and most beautiful rainbow they had ever seen.

All three of the dogs dropped their jaws all at the same time.

They stared out of the window in awe.

This is the most amazing rainbow they had ever seen.

It was enormous and so so bright.

Each color was really vivid.

It was the most perfect rainbow.

The prince noticed they had seen the rainbow.

He said, "Well since you noticed the rainbow, it means I can tell you where I live. If you can see the rainbow, it means you all have a good heart. If you can't see this particular rainbow, it means you are not a good person and don't have a very loving and kind heart."

The only people that can see this rainbow are the people that live in Unitopia.

Unitopia is the prince's home.

It is a very special place.

The only people who can see the rainbow are people with very good hearts.

If you can see the rainbow, if you can ride on the rainbow, you can go to my home to visit Unitopia.

All three of the dogs decided to visit Unitopia.

But before you visit Unitopia, you must rest first.

You must rest because it the best and most magical place to be.

There is so much to do that you are going to need rest.

Everyone snuggles in together on the lovely pillows.

These pillows feel so nice and at home.

Let's all snuggle down and get really really really comfortable.

Let's all sleep and when you wake up you will be there.

Now close your eyes.

Let's relax.
Just go to sleep.
Prince Jack and the dogs all snuggle together on the big soft fluffy pillows.
They have the smoothest and fluffiest blankets that snuggled you just right.
Everyone closed their eyes and adjusted their bodies.
They got nice and comfortable.
They started to take slower and deeper breaths.
Allowing their bodies to start to relax.
Naturally everything was slowing down.
The sounds of the train were mesmerizing and were calming in the background.
It was quiet in the cabin even though the train was so busy and full.
The guard outside was keeping everyone safe.
They relaxed their paws, hooves and legs.
Their bodies got all heavy and sleepy.
Everyone got very very comfortable.
So comfy and sleepy.
Just moving along on the train tracks listening to the white noise of the train.
Everyone relaxed until eventually they fell asleep.
They all slept for the longest time.

The train made a certain movement and a certain noise that gently woke everyone up.
When they looked out of the window, they saw the fantastic beautiful colored rainbow once again.
It had a sign on it that said, "Unitopia Is This Way."
The dogs and their new friend prince Jack bounced off the train after their long nap.
They were so full of energy and so very excited.
What kind of adventures was waiting for them?
Bella was bouncing all over the place.
All the dogs were excited and couldn't contain themselves.
The rainbow is breathtakingly beautiful.
They all walked over and as they got closer the dogs could tell the rainbow was moving.
As they got closer, they could see that it was like a moving walkway.
The rainbow was moving forwards and upwards.
When they got right in front of it, the rainbow stops for them.
It always stops for you right here until you climb onto it.
Everyone stepped on the rainbow and it started to move again.
They started traveling forward and up this amazing rainbow.
They were going higher and higher.

They all looked down and they could see the trees, the train station, and little tiny houses.

Everything was getting smaller and smaller as they moved higher and higher up this magnificent rainbow.

The dogs never been this high before, but the prince assured them they are completely safe.

You can never get hurt on this rainbow.

It is a very special rainbow so just relax and enjoy the ride and the scenery.

They kept going higher and higher until eventually, it felt like they stopped right at the top of the rainbow.

Then the prince all told them to sit down and slide down the rainbow.

They all started to zoom forwards.

It was the biggest and farthest slide that they had ever seen.

They were all smiling and laughing.

They were all zooming down the other side of the rainbow.

The breeze was blowing in their faces.

Their little whiskers were flying all over the place.

Their noses started to get a little cold as well.

It was amazing and everyone was screaming and laughing.

It was like the best roller coaster they had ever been on and when they finally got to the bottom, there was a giant trampoline.
The prince climbed on it first and was going up so high and back down
High and back down.
Boing.
Boing.
Boing.
Boing.
Then the dogs all jumped on the trampoline as well.
This is the best day in their lives.
Now let's move on and visit the very special unicorns.
There are lots of unicorns that live here.
This place is really really big and it is a special place.

Unitopia is a beautiful place full of hills, trees, bright colored flowers that smelled so sweet, and there were unicorns everywhere all just doing their own thing.
They were all different colors, shapes, and sizes.
It was like a magical dreamland and the three dogs were loving every second of it.

When they got to the palace, they went straight into the throne room.

At the far end of the room was the throne.

You could have probably fit hundreds and hundreds of unicorns in this room.

It was so big and fancy.

There were fancy looking chairs.

On the throne was princess Selena and the King and Queen of Unitopia.

All of a sudden the dogs felt a little nervous.

Jack bowed down and said, "Father. Mother. Selena. These are my new friends. They are special dogs because they have good hearts full of love and they saw the rainbow which means they are obviously very special. I thought it would be really nice if they came to Unitopia and they hung out with me for the day or possibly a sleepover."

The King, Queen and Selena all stood up to greet their guests.

"Welcome is it very nice to meet you." says the King. "You are always welcome here. Have fun and enjoy yourselves. Eat, sleep, play. Whatever you need to do our home is your home for as long as you stay here."

The Queen says, "Yes you're so very welcome. The kitchen is that way if you are hungry after your long journey."

Jack explains to Princess Selena that the dogs would love to meet here and would love to know her more. The princess said, "Of course. I'm so happy that you're here and I have so many things I can show you. I have a whole wardrobe of different clothes if that is something you would be interested in seeing. We can do that sometime in the day but for now, let's go play outside. Let's go play in the back garden and I'll show you all the fun things you can do here." Everyone went out into the garden.

The garden was so beautiful and it was also such a lovely day in Unitopia.
The sun was shining down and the sky was so blue with big white fluffy clouds.
There were different unicorns in different areas of the garden all playing together.
They were all doing their own thing.
Some of them were reading books, some of them were practicing flying, and some of them were creating magic.
They all went to a big giant swimming pool.
Around this swimming pool were enormous trees.
The trees were so tall and so big and so green.
These are really cool looking trees.

Hanging from the trees were long vines hanging down.

The prince went over to one of the vines and ran really fast backwards and forwards on the ground, building up speed and momentum, swung from the vine, and splashed down into the pool.

It was a big splash and water flew everywhere.

Water drenched everyone and the prince thought it was so funny.

Selena said, "well that's my brother for you. He is very kind and very sweet but he also likes to play his little tricks on everyone."

The dogs did not mind at all but they absolutely loved it.

The dogs all grabbed the vine and did exactly as the prince.

They ran all back and forth and just let go and dived into the pool.

Now its time to get something to eat.

Everyone is getting hungry and they all started walking back towards the palace.

As they started to get closer and closer to the palace, they started to hear trumpets playing.

The prince said that trumpets only play when there was a celebration or a gathering of some kind that is happening.

When they opened the door to the palace through these big double doors, there was really loud applause and cheering.

There were hundreds and hundreds of unicorns all gathered in the big throne room.

Everyone is cheering for Jack.

The King comes up to the prince and said to him, "It's time son. We've been watching your actions over the last couple of months and you've grown so much. You are kind, loving, very funny and most of all you're kind and loving. You are very brave and noble. It is time you get your wings."

The prince's jaw dropped.

He just looked shocked.

The King, Queen, and Selena all gathered around the Prince and circled around him so that the prince was standing in the middle of them.

They all put their spiral unicorn horns together and then magic happened.

Gold glitter beams of light cascaded all around Jack.

It made the most amazing sounds.

It sounded like angels singing, harps playing and beautiful sounds of angels floating all over Jack.

These sounds were actually coming from Jack's horn.

Then like magic Jack's wings just unfolded and stretched out really wide.

All the unicorns in the throne room gasped in awe.

Jack's wings were the colors of the rainbow and beautiful blue at the tips.

Even his mane, tail and hooves turned a little blue.

He looks like he is sparkling like the stars.

He starts flapping his rainbow unicorn wings up and down.

He looked the happiest he has ever been.

"Thank you father and mother. Thank you Selena" the prince said as he flapped his wings.

All of the unicorns applauded and stomped their hooves.

They all started singing in celebration.

The three dogs thought it was absolutely amazing.

Unitopia is the nicest place in all of the world.

It is the most nicest place you could possibly go.

Everyone here is so loving, calm, pleasant, and happy.

It is everything you would want in the world.

All of these unicorns are very serene, calm, peaceful, caring, loving, conscious and kind.

It is the nicest place these dogs had ever been too.

Jack wanted to try out his wings and wanted to go outside.

Everyone went outside as the sun was coming down.

There was a warm lovely haze across the land.

It was a beautiful golden light that made your heart warm and glow deep inside.

The princess told the dogs to hop on her back and go for a ride as well.

They all agreed and climbed on her back.

All of a sudden, the prince gracefully started to glide off the ground.

The princess also lifted off the ground and they all started flying up into the sky.

They were flying up in the clouds all over Unitopia.

They saw how beautiful the place was from way up in the sky.

There were hills, valleys, trees and forests.

They could see many different colors from all the flowers below.

They also could see many many different unicorns everywhere.

It was the perfect night for flying.

It was not windy.

It was not cold.

The moon was up in the sky and the beautiful moonlight was shining down on them.

The prince and princess were sparkly brightly in the moonlight.

It was very nice to fly in the sky.

It is so quiet up here.

Eventually it was time to come back down.

Everyone gathered in Selena's room.

It was a very big and special room.

Her bed was enormous made of pink quilt, pink pillows and everything else was white.

It was so very clean and bright.

They all settled down on the princess's large bed and it was really soft and fluffy.

As they all settled down on Selena's soft fluffy bed, the princess started to talk.

Close your eyes and settle down.

Get all snugly under the big soft quilt and think of the amazing day you've just had.

How exciting was it?

Seeing new things and meeting new people.

I know I had a wonderful day meeting Bella, Jake and Lucy.

I want you all to know that you are now my friends. You are welcome here anytime you wish.

Now all of you take a nice deep breath in and now slowly and gently let it out.
You feel so happy and relaxed.
Remember how high you flew up in the sky?
Remember how lovely that feeling is.
How the wind felt on your face.
Take another deep breathe in and slowly let it out.
When you feel so sleepy.
Now one last time, take another deep breath in and then slowly let it out.
Even though your eyes are closed they feel ever so tired.
You're breathing soft and gently now.
Each time you breathe in you take in the good thoughts and positive feelings.
You're beginning to drift in and out of sleep as you sink deeper and deeper into the lovely soft and squishy quilt.
You smile peacefully to yourself and feel every so happy.
You know that in life, you can be anything you want to be.

You know that you are a truly special person with a loving heart.
You are so loved and you are so protected and you are so very very safe here in Unitopia.

You hear a tapping on the window and you wonder what it could be.
You go over and take a look.
You see a lovely little robin has landed on your window ledge.
He is holding a white envelope in his beak.
He gives it you and flies off.
You open the envelope and you see that it is an invitation with your name on it.
It says we hereby invite you to Unitopia Summer Festival.
It has your name written in fancy golden letters on it.
You are so excited you jump up and down with delight.
Do you remember how to get there?
You have to close your eyes again and breathe in deeply and slowly.
Breath out.
Now breathe in.

Then breathe out.
Breath in and breath out.

Now imagine yourself sitting in a large green field.
The sun is shining brightly, and it is a very beautiful clear day outside.
You can see for miles and miles and miles.
As you look up at the sky you see a beautiful rainbow of all different colors.
The colors are so bright and so clear.
You can see each color in the rainbow.
You recognize this rainbow.
It is the same rainbow to Unitopia!

You go over and you stop at the beginning of the rainbow and it stops moving for you.
You step on it and as soon as you do, it begins to move again.
As it moves forward it also begins to climb higher and higher and higher.
You can touch the colors of the rainbow.
You can feel the colors of the rainbow.
Can you feel them?

The rainbow goes higher still, and you can see the field below you.
Can you see it?
The rainbow now reaches the topmost part and then it begins to move back down again.
It is starting to get a little slippery now so you sit down and you begin to slide.
You are sliding down the rainbow!
It is like a great big waterslide with beautiful colors all around you.
You are going faster and faster!
The wind is whipping through your hair making it fly everywhere.
This makes you laugh out loud and you are laughing so hard your tummy starts to hurt.
You can now see the end of the rainbow and it is coming up fast.
You notice at the bottom of the rainbow is a huge trampoline.
You love this part.
You hit the trampoline so fast you bounce right back up again.
Oh my!
This is so much fun!
You start bouncing some more for a little bit and now you decide to get off the trampoline.
You decide to go search for the summer festival.

As you walk, you instantly see the princess unicorn Selena.
She is with her friends to welcome you back and take you to the summer festival!

She can not wait to show you the amazing summer festival.
She is so happy and delighted you could make it.
You start walking with the princess and her friends.
When you arrive, you hear the sound of wonderful music playing.
There are fairy lights everywhere.
There are also big flashing lights.
You are absolutely amazed by everything you see here.
There are fantastic carnival rides.
Roller coasters are dipping in and out of the clouds.
Unicorn races are happening in the sky.
You can see them flash and run past above you.
This is so fantastic!
There is live music playing and it looks like a gnome is dancing and playing the guitar.
It is a whole band of gnomes!
One is singing in the background; one is playing the drums and one playing the piano.

This is all absolutely wonderful!

There are huge balloons everywhere and so much candy everywhere!

There are so many different carnival games.

There is also a water park!

There are so many different stalls to buy amazing things.

Whatever you want, they have it here at the summer festival.

For a little while more, explore this amazing place with the princess unicorn and her friends.

Go and have lots of fun.

Try all the different games and rides.

Try all of the amazing foods because it smells so yummy.

Spend the rest of the afternoon with your unicorn friends.

Maybe you can find something here to take back home with you.

Maybe something to just remember this amazing day.

Now it is time for you to return home.

It is time for you to leave Unitopia and the wonderful summer festival.

You can always come back next year.
You say goodbye to your friends and return to the beautiful rainbow.
You step aboard and it rises and rises.
You feel so peaceful and relaxed.
You feel so happy and calm and very tired now.
You keep traveling along the amazing rainbow and just thinking about your amazing day.
How wonderful it was to see the princess unicorn and her friends again.
You reach the highest point of the rainbow and you begin to slide down the other side.
You feel so good, happy and sleepy now.
You have had such an amazing day, but it is time for you to sleep.
You are now back in your bed relaxing.
You are back in your warm soft bed.
You can feel your mind is sliding down into a deep deep sleep.

Just rest now and have the best night ever.
You can return anytime you wish.
Now imagine yourself sitting in a large green field.
The sun is shining brightly, and it is such a beautiful clear day.

You can see for miles and miles around you.
You feel very calm and very relaxed and very very peaceful.
You can hear the birds singing to each other.
Can you hear them?

As you look up into the sky you see a beautiful rainbow of many different colors.
The colors are so bright and so clear.
Can you see the beautiful rainbow?
Can you see the colors shining brightly?
The colors look as though they are alive with so much vibrancy and energy.
You are drawn to this rainbow.
When you walk towards it, you feel your steps becoming lighter and lighter.
As you get closer you begin to float, and your feet are not even touching the ground anymore!
Then you realize where you are.
This is the magnificent rainbow to Unitopia!
The rainbow stops moving and you step on it.
Then it starts moving and you begin to climb higher and higher.
You can now touch the colors of the rainbow.
Can you feel it?

As the rainbow goes higher, you can see the fields below you.

You can see the trees and birds flying.

There are a couple of birds flying past you and the rainbow.

When the rainbow reaches the topmost part, you sit down and start to slide.

It is like a such a wonderful colorful waterslide.

There are beautiful colors all around you and you go faster and faster.

The wind is whipping through your hair and making it fly everywhere.

This makes you laugh out loud so much and you are laughing so much it is making your tummy hurt.

You always love this part of the journey to Unitopia.

The end of the rainbow is coming up fast and you can see the huge trampoline.

Then with a great big leap, you bounce off the trampoline and land softly in the beautiful green meadow.

You look around and you can see unicorns everywhere.

They all see you and come to greet you and welcome you back.

They are so pleased that you have come back to vist them again.

They are very magical beings and they always know the truth of things.

They know the truth of you and you are so beautiful to them

All the unicorns speak at once and they say, "Hello! How are you?"

They talk so much that you don't know who to answer first.

Then all of a sudden, they all stop talking and bow their heads to a different unicorn.

This unicorn comes out from the rest of them and she has very silky, very shiny and has a sparkling magical horn.

She is the princess Unicorn and she gives you the biggest smile and says she misses you.

You can see the love in her eyes.

No matter different we may look from each other, she only sees the beautiful person you truly are.

You see her diamond encrusted spiral horn with pink crystals.

You see her beautiful silver mane with sparkles of pink on it.

You can see her sparkling silver hooves as she walks so softly and her hooves make no sound at all.

Her horn is the most powerful out of all the unicorn horns.
She has the strongest one with magical healing qualities.
The gentle breeze of wind blows past her heart and it produces the most beautiful flute like melody.
It sounds so wonderful and soothing to you.
It is so peaceful.
So calming.
The princess tells you that she is glad and so very happy you have come to see her again.
She tells you that this is a very special day.
She says that she has the power to grant you a gift so rare for this one day.
It is a gift no other person has been granted before.
Today she has the power to let you become a unicorn.
She has the power to let you really feel what it is like to be a unicorn.

She asks you if you would like to experience this and you say, "Yes of course!"
The princess unicorn bows one leg and tilts her head towards you and something amazing occurs.
Her beautiful spiral horn begins to shimmer and shine.

Tiny particles of golden dust begin to come from the sky above you and it gently begins to surround you. It surrounds your whole body and it feels so nice and peaceful.

It is so tingly, warm and relaxing.

Tiny particles of golden dust surrounds all of you.

You feel your body beginning to change.

You feel your legs and arms turning into a unicorn!

Oh my goodness!

You feel a beautiful long tail growing.

A mane that shimmers and shines and then suddenly you feel something happening to your back.

You feel wings growing there.

Oh my goodness!

You have wings and you stretch them out wide.

They feel so fantastic.

The princess smiles happily and graciously to you.

With sparkles coming from her eyes she asks you if you would like to fly with her.

You say oh yes please!

You both turn and gallop together and you begin to fly with each other.

You can feel your wings flapping in the breeze.

You can feel all the muscles in your body moving as one.
Now all of the other unicorns start flying with you as well!
When the princess moves left or right everyone follows her.
It is like all of you have become one.
It is like you guys all are working together.
You can even hear and feel what the other unicorns are feeling and thinking too!
You are completely one with them.
For a few moments, be a unicorn.
Just be a unicorn and fly as a unicorn.
Most of all enjoy what it is like to be one with them.
Feel the breeze on your face and mane.
Be a unicorn.

Now it is time for you to return home.
It is time for you to leave Unitopia.
You gently land back down and as you do, you feel your body return to the normal you.
You feel absolutely amazing.
You feel so grateful for a chance to really fly with the unicorns.
It was so fun to actually be one of them.

You thank the princess for giving you this very special gift today.
You say goodbye to everyone.
You wave and you smile, and you turn to go.
The unicorns teach us to always believe in ourselves.

You feel so sleepy now after your amazing day with the unicorns.
So sleepy now that your eyes have already closed.
You think to yourself that you are so lucky to have such wonderful friends.
You are drifting deeper and deeper now into sleep.
You will have the most wonderful night sleep ever.
Just snuggle down, maybe turn over on your side.
You feel so safe, so protected, and so very very loved.
When you wake up in the morning, you will feel completely refreshed bright and alert.
You feel so very ready to begin the new day.

CHAPTER 7

Great Undersea Friends

Make yourself comfortable.
Lay down on your sofa or bed.
Now tense up all of your muscles and hold it for a few seconds.
Then let it all go allowing your arms and legs to go nice and limp.
Not breath in deeply really filling your lungs with air.
Now breathe out slowly and gently releasing all that air from your lungs.

Breathe in again slowly and deeply.
Hold your breath just for a moment and breathe out.

One more time, deep breathe in and breathe out.
Every time you breathe in, your body becomes more and more relaxed.
Fill your body up.
You are going to feel very loose and very soft as you just breathe in and breath out.
Breathe in and breathe out.

Now imagine you are standing on a beautiful golden sandy beach.
You can hear the wonderful sounds of the waves as they come up onto the sand.
You can even smell the ocean spray.
That lovely ocean spray you can only find at the beach.
You take your shoes off now and your socks.
You start walking on the warm golden sand towards the water and you feel that beneath your feet.
It feels so lovely and so warm.

Now push your toes deep into the sand.
Feel it in between your toes.
Does it feel soft and warm?

Or does it feel big and rough?

You look around you and you realize that the beach is so wide and long.

It stretches out for miles ahead and it is so sunny and warm here.

It is so warm and sunny that it makes you feel so special inside.

You feel so safe and so calm and so peaceful.

You walk over to the water's edge and put your feet in the water.

It feels so nice, so cool and so refreshing.

The water splashes over your ankles just a tiny bit.

Suddenly you hear something behind you.

You turn around and to see what it is.

It is a boy about your age.

He has blonde hair with big blue eyes.

He has the biggest grin on his face too!

He shouts and motions you to come over.

He tells you his name is Adam.

He has come to play soccer on the beach with his friends

He asks if you want to play too.

Well of course you say yes.

You love soccer!

You look around but you do not see anyone else on the beach.

Adam gives a little laugh and tells you he is waiting for his friendly friend the shark.

The shark's name is Henry.

He is Adam's friend and lives in the sea.

He is not just an ordinary shark. He is actually a magical shark.

Adam reaches in his pocket for a whistle.

This is a magical whistle that he uses to call Henry.

Henry has a very good sense of hearing.

He can hear this whistle from miles away.

Adams puts the whistle to his mouth and gives it a big blow.

Henry will be here soon Adam says.

You suddenly see a fin pop up just above the waves.

Then you see Henry's head pop up and looks really big in the waves!

You hope Henry is not hungry now.

You wonder how on earth are you going to play soccer with a shark?

They do not have any feet.

You look at Henry and he has sparkling magical dust floating around him all over in the water.

It looks so amazing but you can't seem to see where it is coming from.

Then the most astonishing thing happens.

Henry walks out of the water with two legs and two feet!

Your mouth drops wide open.
A shark is walking on the beach out of the water!
He is also wearing bright yellow shorts and soccer shoes.
Adam tells you he only grows legs when you come on land and especially to play soccer, but when he goes back into sea he will turn back into a normal shark.
Adam tells you he doesn't eat people so don't worry.
Henry actually loves fruits and vegetables!

Henry puts on his goggles and says alright, let's play some football!
You will be on offense and Adam can play on defense and Henry will be the goalkeeper.
For a few moments, you play soccer with Henry and Adam.
Just have fun on this wonderful golden sandy beach.
See if you can try score some goals.

Wow! That was so fun!
Did you score a goal?
Henry asks if you would like to meet his brother Bruce.

Well of course you say yes.
Henry tells you can ride on his back in the sea and just hold onto his fin underwater.
He says he has spare goggles for you to put on.
He then sprinkles you with golden magic dust.
This is so you can breathe underwater!
You are absolutely amazed by this!
Harry swims far out into sea and dives down deep into the water.
You can see fish swimming past you.
One of them takes off his little cup and says good morning and swims off.
You see all of the underwater sea creatures just all floating and swimming around.
What else can you see down here?
What can you see under the water?
Then you see a house underwater.
It is Henry's house!
This is where he lives and Bruce is waiting at the doorway.
Bruce gives a big grin and says hello to you.
He asks if you would like to have a strawberry smoothie.
You go inside and you say hello to his mom and dad.
The dad's name is Will and his mom's name is Emma.
You finish your smoothie and Bruce suggests that you show you around where they live.

Maybe some of their other friends will be out playing as well.
You meet their crab friend named Dotty.
She is such a friendly crab.
She is sitting on a rock knitting with bright pink yarn.
She is wearing glasses perched on the end of her nose.
She tells you she is knitting a scarf to go with her brand new hat.
Henry tells you that Dotty is his best friend.
They go everywhere together.
She is also teaching Henry to knit.
Just for a little while, go see and explore with Henry, Bruce and Dotty.

Maybe you guys can play volleyball.
Dotty loves that.
Maybe you can just swim around to your heart's content.
Whatever you want to do you can make happen in this magical underwater place.

Now that you have seen where all your new friends live, Henry asks if you would like to stay at his house tonight.
In fact, he says everyone can.
How wonderful!
You get to have a sleepover with a very friendly shark with all his friends and family too.
Go back to Henry's house and you all go into his bedroom.
To your surprise, there is a bed for everyone.
Dotty finds herself the softest bed and climbs on it.
You all find your own beds and settle down nicely.
You do feel rather sleep now.
You had a pretty amazing day playing soccer with Adam and a shark that can grow legs.
Your eyes begin to feel very heavy and very sleepy now.
Your eyelids are beginning to droop.
Your body feels so peaceful, so relaxed, so calm and so very very heavy now.
You feel ever so happy.
You close your eyes and just listen to the sounds of the ocean.
You feel your breathing as it begins to slow down.
Your chest is gently rising and falling.
You take a deep breath in gently and slowly breathe out.

Listen to the gentle sounds of the ocean.
It is time for you to rest for a beautiful restful sleep.
You go deeper and deeper into sleep.
When you wake up in the morning, you will be back in your very own bed.

Conclusion

Thank you so much for listening to *Bedtime Sleep Meditations For Children.*

I hope this book has helped you have lots of wonderful dreams and amazing nights of sleep.

If you ever find yourself stressed out, angry, overwhelmed or sad, you can always refer to this book's teachings and re-listen to it again.

If you enjoyed this book and if it has helped you have a better night's sleep, be sure to leave a thoughtful review on Amazon of how this book has helped you. This is so more kids like you can have amazing sleeps every night!

Thank you again for listening to this book and I wish you all the love, happiness and amazing nights of sleep ahead!